*What Time It is?*

*Denise Renner*

# Do you know What time It is?

Denise Renner

Harrison House

*Do You Know What Time It Is?*
ISBN: 978-0-9725454-8-8
Copyright © 2006 by Denise Renner
P. O. Box 702040
Tulsa, OK 74170-2040

2  3  4  5  6  /  25 24 23 22
2nd Printing

Editorial Consultant: Cynthia D. Hansen
Text Design: Lisa Simpson
SimpsonProductions.net

# Table of Contents

# Introduction

There is nothing sadder than a life lived but wasted. Each person born on this earth is made in the image of God and created to do great things; yet so many live out their lives without ever fulfilling a fraction of what God created them to do. Putting off till tomorrow what God is telling them to do today, people waste day after day, week after week, year after year — until suddenly, they realize that there *is* no more time left for them to obey.

It is a very dangerous thing not to count our time as precious and very valuable. We are all given 24 hours in a day, but it is our choice what we do with that time. The clock is ticking, and every single breath in our lungs is a gift. As long as we are breathing, we still have time to make our lives count for something, to give our lives for someone else, to serve other people.

We need to face the fact that there is a funeral in our future if Jesus doesn't come first and that it's up to us to decide what we do with the time we have remaining on this earth. If we waste that time, we won't be able to blame it on someone else, for God has given all of us the power to make choices. It is our choice what enters into our minds; it is our choice what comes out of our mouths; and it is our choice what we do with our time.

Proverbs 1:5 says, *"A wise man will hear, and will increase learning; and a man of understanding shall attain unto wise counsels...."* I believe what I am saying to you in this book is the counsel of the Lord. These are crucial times we live in, and how we spend our time is a very serious matter. We *must* take the opportunity we have available right now to do what God has

8

# Introduction

called us to do, because the clock is ticking, and time is passing us by.

I pray that as you read this book, your heart will be stirred to stop wasting precious time and to start obeying what God has already asked you to do. That is the only way you will be ready for the wonderful future He desires to unfold in your life!

*Denise Renner*

# 1

## 'Sleep On,
## And Take Your Rest'

Every single one of us has allotted times for different seasons or assignments in our lives. In each of these seasons, the allotted time comes, and then it goes — and when that time is over, there is usually no way to get it back.

Now, I am a woman of faith, and I do believe that God redeems the time. But

I'm talking about a dangerous attitude we often nurture in our lives that says, "Oh, I'll do that tomorrow. I don't need to be in a hurry; my situation isn't so bad." And we keep on saying that as the days and months and years go by. Then all of a sudden, we look back and realize that the clock has run out for that particular season or assignment that God had given to us. The allotted time we had is gone. We wasted that time because we didn't take it seriously. And we ask in despair, "Where did the time go?"

> **I'm talking about a dangerous attitude we often nurture in our lives that says, "Oh, I'll do that tomorrow."**

# 'Sleep On, and Take Your Rest'

The Lord may speak to our hearts and say:

- ❖ "I want you to do something about your health."
- ❖ "I want you to spend more time in prayer and the Word every day."
- ❖ "I want you to witness to your neighbor."
- ❖ "I want you to further your education."
- ❖ "I want you to start exercising regularly."

And too often we respond with these kinds of answers:

- ❖ "Lord, I don't want to do that."
- ❖ "Lord, I just don't have time!"
- ❖ "Lord, you know how I love Coke!"

❖ "Lord, I have so many lunch-
eons and banquets to
attend. How in the world
could I ever fast?"

We give excuse after excuse after excuse,
and the hours tick by; the days tick by; the
weeks tick by; the months tick by; the years
tick by. Finally, the time comes when we
are no longer able to do the thing that God
asked us to do.

## The Disciples' Missed Opportunity

In Matthew 26:36-46, we see that the
three disciples who were closest to Jesus
missed their allotted time to help Him in
His hour of greatest need:

**Then cometh Jesus with them
unto a place called Gethsemane,
and saith unto the disciples, Sit ye
here, while I go and pray yonder.**

And he took with him Peter and the two sons of Zebedee, and began to be sorrowful and very heavy.

Then saith he unto them, My soul is exceeding sorrowful, even unto death: tarry ye here, and watch with me.

And he went a little further, and fell on his face, and prayed, saying, O my Father, if it be possible, let this cup pass from me: nevertheless not as I will, but as thou wilt.

And he cometh unto the disciples, and findeth them asleep, and saith unto Peter, What, could ye not watch with me one hour?

Watch and pray, that ye enter not into temptation: the spirit indeed is willing, but the flesh is weak.

He went away again the second time, and prayed, saying, O my Father, if this cup may not pass away from me, except I drink it, thy will be done.

And he came and found them asleep again: for their eyes were heavy.

And he left them, and went away again, and prayed the third time, saying the same words.

Then cometh he to his disciples, and saith unto them, SLEEP ON NOW, AND TAKE YOUR REST: behold, the hour is at hand, and the Son of man is betrayed into the hands of sinners.

Rise, let us be going: behold, he is at hand that doth betray me.

One day I was reading this passage of Scripture, and I was captivated by Jesus' words in verse 45: *"...Sleep on now, and take your rest....*" It hit my heart that, at that moment, the allotted time given to the three disciples to pray for Jesus and to help Him in His time of need *was gone*. At that point, the only thing Jesus could say to them was, "Sleep on now."

The disciples had been offered such a unique opportunity. I don't know of another place in the Scriptures where Jesus asked for personal help and attention from His disciples. Never before in history and never again would Jesus make this particular request. The burden He felt was so heavy that He couldn't even go very far from the other three before He fell to the ground in agony. Jesus was deep in the throes of the struggle for which He was born — to bear the sins, the sicknesses, and the poverty of all humanity — and He was saying *yes* to the Father's will.

Jesus was having to say *yes* to being separated from God His Father; *yes* to bearing God's wrath for the punishment of our sins; *yes* to enduring not only death on the Cross, but hell itself. It was time for the sinless Son of God to become the spotless Lamb that was slain to bear the sins of the world. And for this one crucial hour — when Jesus would suffer such mental and emotional anguish that He would sweat drops of blood — He was asking His closest friends, *"Would you please pray with Me?"*

Three times Jesus asked Peter, James, and John to watch and pray with Him in His hour of need. Yet each time Jesus came back to them, He found them sleeping. Then His time of prayer was over, and the disciples' opportunity to stand with Him in prayer was gone. They would never have that opportunity again. Jesus was never going to suffer like that again. He would never again be in the Garden of

Gethsemane, pouring out His heart and His life before the world.

These three disciples had blown their opportunity. They had missed their allotted time. Jesus didn't have His closest friends' prayers to help Him during His time of intense need because they fell asleep. So when He returned to them and saw that they were sleeping, Jesus sadly said to the three men, "Go ahead and sleep; take your rest. Behold, the hour is at hand, and the Son of Man is betrayed into the hands of the sinners."

> **These three disciples had blown their opportunity. They had missed their allotted time.**

I had read this passage many times through the years, but when I read it this particular day, the importance of *time* hit me in the face. I realized in a way I never had before that there is an allotted time for us to do the different things God asks us to do. And when that time is gone, the opportunity to fulfill a particular assignment is lost and, more often than not, can never be regained again.

> There is an allotted time for us to do the different things God asks us to do.

### The Suddenness Of Time Cut Short

The day this scripture hit me so hard was soon after the tsunami had devastated the countries bordering the Indian Ocean in December 2004. I already knew that hundreds of thousands of people had lost their lives in that horrible tragedy, and I was struck with how suddenly time had run out for so many. Those hundreds of thousands of people didn't wake up that morning thinking, *I'm going to die today, so I'd better get ready.* And the people who lost loved ones in the tsunami didn't wake up that day and say, "My loved one is going to die today, so I'd better show him [or her] more appreciation!"

No, one moment those men and women and children were breathing, and the next they were in eternity. They had no clue and no warning that their time on this earth was about to be cut short.

I want to share another example of time suddenly cut short that hits very close to home for me. In November 2004, two young women who attended our seminary, ages 20 and 21, were killed instantly by a train after making a very foolish mistake.

There is a certain place in the Moscow railway system where many people break the rules by crossing the tracks in order to save themselves the ten-minute walk around the tracks. That day these two girls did the same foolish thing that so many others do, trying to save a little time. But they were late in starting over the tracks, so when the next oncoming train came through at 60 miles an hour, these two young women were trapped in the tiny space between the train track and the wall with nowhere to run. All they could do was stand back as far as they could — but to no avail. As the train barreled through the passage, the young women were hit and killed instantly.

Those two young women didn't expect that outcome. They didn't wake up that morning believing that they were going to die. They didn't know their time on earth was about to be over. They were healthy and full of life one day — and standing before Jesus the next.

I'll tell you something else about that tragedy. The night before it happened, one of those young women had gotten stuck in a restroom, unable to get the door open. During that experience, she received the revelation in her heart that her life was valuable and not to be wasted. She even shared that revelation with some of the people close to her.

That was the Holy Spirit warning this young woman to be on guard and to proceed carefully through the coming days — but she didn't take heed. Otherwise, she wouldn't have put her life in needless jeopardy by trying to cross those tracks!

## The Peril Of Putting Things Off

Now, I'm not saying we should be afraid that we might die at any moment or that someone we love is going to die. Certainly we should have faith to live long and strong on this earth. But what about those people who are not walking with God? What about those who are not standing in faith for a long life? What if they pass our way and we don't even open our mouths about Jesus or try to do anything for them — and then later we hear, "Did you know that So-and-so died?"

I'm in my middle-age years now, and one thing I've started to notice is that a lot of my life has already passed by. And although many wonderful things have happened in my life as I've followed the Lord, I know there are certain things God has asked me to do that I have *not* done because I put them off. I kept thinking, *I'll do it tomorrow. I have time to wait* — until it was too late.

For example, many years ago when my husband Rick and I had just started ministering on the road, I had a dream that I knew was from the Lord. I dreamed of a young man with whom I went to high school — a good friend I hadn't thought of in many years. In my dream, this young man was dying of AIDS.

My first faithless thought was, *What can I do? Surely there is nothing I can do.* So what do you think I did? *I did nothing.* I didn't even pray!

Three months went by. Then one day I was visiting my little hometown of Miami, Oklahoma, and I happened to read the obituaries in the local newspaper. There it was — the name of the young man I had dreamed about. The newspaper said he had died of a long-term illness at home.

I didn't know it on the night God gave me that dream, but I had three months — *and only three months* — to act on what He had shown me. The clock was ticking; the days and weeks were passing by. Then came the day of the young man's death, and my time to obey was over. God had wanted to reach out to my high school friend through me, but I had done nothing.

Something similar happened the night before those two young women were killed in that train accident. Many of their fellow Bible school students woke up in the middle of the night and couldn't get back to sleep. The Holy Spirit was alerting them to pray to avert a tragedy, but none of them picked up on His quiet leading. Not one of them spent time that night in prayer.

God is trying to save us. He is trying to save our children and our neighbors. But we hinder His ability to work in a situation where time is critical if He has to wait for us to obey. We have to change our attitude about *time*.

Too often we act like we have all the time we need, anytime we want it. We act like everyone we love is going to live a long time and we can therefore take him or her for granted.

But we need to be wise about what we do with our time. The Bible says that our lives are like a vapor (James 4:14).

Psalm 103:15,16 says the same thing a different way: *"As for man, his days are as grass: as a flower of the field, so he flourisheth. For the wind passeth over it, and it is gone; and the place thereof shall know it no more."*

Our time on this earth is limited, and the Lord has already numbered our days, ordaining good works for us to walk in. So let it never be said of us that Jesus found us sleeping on our

**Our time on this earth is limited, and God has already numbered our days, ordaining good works for us to walk in.**

watch. Let Him never have reason to say, "Your opportunity has been lost. Sleep on, and take your rest"!

# 2

# Don't Waste Your Allotted Time

Time is even more precious than money (if you can imagine that!). You can always get more money, but it is impossible to regain time once it is gone. Time runs out, and you can't get it back.

Now, I know the Word of God says that He restores the years the locusts have eaten (Joel 2:25) and helps us redeem the time (Ephesians 5:16). Thank God for His mercy in doing this for us! God's Word is absolutely the truth, but these questions remain: What is our attitude toward the precious time God gives us? Are we obeying Him when He speaks to us and asks us to do something? Or do we say, "I'll do it tomorrow; I don't need to be in a hurry. I've got plenty of time"?

**What is our attitude toward the precious time God gives us?**

We go through many seasons in our lives, and in each season, God calls us to do particular things. We'd better make sure we're taking full advantage of each season by bearing the fruit we're supposed to bear in that specific time in our lives. If we miss the opportunity to produce during a given season, that same opportunity may never come again once that period of time in our lives is over.

# Don't Waste Your Allotted Time

Perhaps you're supposed to start a business, but you're afraid to take the risk. Maybe there are new places you're supposed to go or new people you need to meet, but you'd rather stay put in the comfortable status quo.

I remember years ago when God asked me to start a women's Bible study, and my first step of obedience was to meet with the pastor and get his blessing and permission. For me, this was the hard part. I loved this pastor and respected him and his wife so much. But in the past whenever I had the opportunity to talk to him, I'd find myself stumbling over my words, saying dumb things, and looking very insecure (which I was). Now I had to go to dinner with the pastor and his family and share my idea about starting a women's Bible study in our home!

This was a *huge* deal to me, because I had no idea what I would say. To me, it was like Star Wars — and I was the one entering into unknown territory! I was so scared!

You see, my pastor and his wife were wonderful people. They were not the problem in this situation — the problem was inside *me*. God was requiring me to face my fear and leave my comfort zone.

When we went to dinner, I was wringing my hands through the entire meal, and I hardly ate a bite. Finally, dinner was almost over and everyone was eating their dessert. I thought to myself, *Denise, you've got to do it! You've got to ask him! It's now or never! Ask right now!*

I opened my mouth and, with voice shaking, I said, "Pastor, God has put it on my heart to hold a women's Bible study in our home two times a month. I want to teach women how to love their husbands and their children according to Titus 2:4 and 5."

# Don't Waste Your Allotted Time

As I waited for his answer, I thought, *What will he say? Do I look foolish or presumptuous, thinking that I can lead a Bible study?*

But my pastor's response was immediate and simple. He warmly said, "Denise, I think that would be great!" I almost fainted!

I led that Bible study for two years, and it was well attended. We even held a conference for all the women of the church, and more than 200 women came! In addition, from that group of women who attended the Bible study, four answered the call to full-time ministry!

I didn't know it at the time when God called me to lead the women's Bible study, but that space of two years was my allotted time for the Bible study. Two years later, He would call our family to leave America and begin our ministry in the former Soviet Union. If I hadn't climbed out of my comfort zone and said *yes* to the Lord, I would have missed my season for fulfilling that particular assignment from Heaven.

*You see, you have to seize and use the time you have now.* You run a high risk of losing your opportunity if you say, "I'm going to do it next year." By this time next year, the allotted time to do what is on your heart may have come and gone!

> **You run a high risk of losing your opportunity if you say, "I'm going to do it next year."**

### The Season of Teaching the Word To Our Children

Let me give you an important example of what I'm talking about. There is an allotted time for us to teach the Word to our young children. We should take full advantage of this season, for we have a priceless opportunity to nurture young minds and hearts in the ways of the Lord. It is crucial that we plan our time wisely and make any sacrifice necessary in order to sow the Word into our little ones.

When our children are little, their hearts and minds are open and pliable. That is the specially allotted time God has given to us to plant the Word and its principles of truths into their young hearts. They are like young tree seedlings trying to take root and grow in rich soil.

> **There is an allotted time for us to teach the Word to our young children.**
>
>

A little seedling is so young and tender. It receives nourishment from the sun and rain and welcomes the tender care given by the gardener on its way to becoming strong and fruitful. But when that season of growing is over and the young tree has become strong on its own, it is no longer dependent, pliable, and tender. The time has passed for all the nurturing and tender care.

As it is with young tree seedlings, so it is with our children. When they are young, their little hearts are tender and we are better able to mold them according to the Word of God. But as they grow older, their hearts may not be as pliable as they were when they were five or eight or eleven years old. They begin to form their own opinions and may become less willing to listen to our counsel.

When the season of planting and watering the Word of God in our children's lives has passed, it is too late to start the nurturing that should have happened years ago. That season only comes once. We must plant, water, strengthen, nourish, and pull out as many weeds as we can while our children are young, for this season will be over before we know it.

# Don't Waste Your Allotted Time

Too many times, parents wish away this season when their children are young, thinking, *I feel like my freedom has been stolen from me. I used to have such an exciting life. I can't wait till the kids go to school or are grown and move out of the house so I can be on my own and do what I want to do.*

**If you are a parent with young children, I beg you to receive this counsel.**

You need to enjoy this season of raising your children. They're going to grow up so quickly! When they're young, they believe everything that comes out of our mouths. They treasure all the attention you give them. Their hearts are so tender. That is the time to plant the Word of God in their hearts. You must not let that time pass by without taking full advantage of it!

If you have the attitude, "I'll start doing that next week" or "I'll do it next month," you will never do it. Then one day your little ones will become teenagers, and they won't have the strong foundation of the Word in them that they need to live as successful, God-fearing adults.

*If you're a mother, I want to specifically address you here.* God has given you a very powerful position in your home as the mother. Proverbs 14:1 says, *"Every wise woman buildeth her house: but the foolish plucketh it down with her hands."* That means you have the power to make your home or break it — to make it a happy home or one full of sadness and regret.

You carry the entire emotional atmosphere in your home. And you were designed by God to give your children exactly what they need.

You may have said to yourself, *My husband should take the spiritual leadership in teaching the Word to the children, so I'm going to wait for him to do it.* But you need to take advantage of the privilege God has given *you* to teach your children. Don't put off the entire responsibility on your husband and lose your opportunity to see your little ones grow up strong in the Word. You do what *you're* supposed to do.

Get into the habit of putting the Word into your children, even while they are still infants. Then when they become teenagers, your children's hearts will still be soft to receive from the Word of God.

**Get into the habit of putting the Word into your children, even while they are still infants.**

And understand this: The devil will try to take you down every possible detour that might keep you from doing what you are supposed to do in raising your children. For instance, he'll orchestrate a situation where you get offended at a sister or brother in the church, hoping that you'll then spend the next three years stewing over that offense. The enemy loves it when that happens! He wants to steal your time through offense so that you waste five or six years hardened by unforgiveness; meanwhile, your young children will be growing up without a strong knowledge of the Word!

The Bible says that the cares of this life will steal the Word out of your heart if you're not careful: *"And the cares of this world, and the deceitfulness of riches, and the lusts of other things entering in, choke the Word, and it becometh unfruitful"* (Mark 4:19). But you don't have to allow yourself to stay offended. Take the time to seek God with all your heart, and get free of any offense. (I recommend my little book *Gift of Forgiveness* to help you in this struggle.) Then get back to teaching and planting the Word into your children's young hearts. Don't let the devil steal three or four or five years from you by yielding to the power of offense.

Parents who fall for the devil's strategies — wishing away their children's younger years, getting distracted by offense, or spending too much time on less important hobbies or pursuits — often neglect this all-important responsibility of teaching their children the Word. And as the years go by and their children grow older, wrong attitudes that come straight from the world begin to form and harden in the young people's hearts.

This process is so dangerous, for there is a powerful evil force in this world, applying great pressure on our children as it uses its corrupt influence to try to form, shape, and mold them into the world's image. This is the spirit of antichrist, and it is operating in the world today. This spirit is against everything godly, and it is pumping its ideas into children's minds much more quickly than the Church is planting God's truth into their hearts. As a result, there has been an explosion of godless people who embrace a complete absence of morals and live by very low standards (if any at all).

I am absolutely shocked by what I see when I return to minister in the United States each year. I have a different outlook than most Americans do because I've lived in the former Soviet Union for so many years and am looking in from the outside. For instance, I'm appalled at the way sexual immorality is so casually accepted in America. The world presents premarital sex as no big deal — on the same level as going out and having a cup of coffee with someone!

So many of today's youth — young people who still don't know the end from the beginning and have hardly begun to live — are giving away their virginity freely and with little thought of the consequences. As a result, America has an epidemic of teenage pregnancies; more than one million unborn babies are aborted every year; and sexually transmitted diseases are on the rise. And I'm just talking about this one area of sexual purity among our young people!

The enemy is pouring immorality into the modern youth culture from every direction — through the media, through music, even through the educational system. He is bombarding young people's minds with the message, *This is normal. Chill out. Don't get so upset about the whole thing. Do what you feel like doing!* As a result, the world's way of thinking is flooding into this young generation's hearts and minds.

That is why we must make sure that we are doing all we can do to pour the Word of God into our own children while they are young. When they reach the age of 17 or 18, their hearts may not be as tender and open to our words.

I am not saying this to condemn you if your children have already grown up and you aren't seeing good fruit produced in their lives. I am writing this because it's the truth and an important warning to parents who are still raising their young children.

If you are one of these mothers or fathers, I want to encourage you to give yourself to the training of your children in the admonition of the Lord, realizing that this season of your life only comes once.

> **Give yourself to the training of your children in the admonition of the Lord, realizing that this season of your life only comes once.**

# Don't Waste Your Allotted Time

## Stand in Faith for Your Children
## In Prayer

Maybe you missed your season of raising your children under the Word of God because you weren't saved when they were young or for some other reason. As a result of this lack of foundation in the Word, your adult children may be experiencing problems in their lives right now. If this is your situation, you are now in another season — *the season of intercession.* This is also a very important season — one that is well worth the sacrifice of your time and effort.

Don't let someone else do your interceding for you. Whether your children are young adolescents, teenagers, or broken-hearted adults, it is your responsibility to carry them before the throne of God. Take advantage of the time allotted to you, for this is your season to relentlessly intercede for them and to say, "Lord, I *refuse* to let my children escape Your Presence. I declare in Jesus' name that every one of my children *will* serve You. I plead the blood of Jesus over them; I stand in the gap for them; and I will not cease to bring them before Your throne."

My husband Rick teaches some crucial truths regarding this issue of relentlessly standing in prayer for a desired answer. His words are especially significant to those of us who are parents as we pray for the fulfillment of God's purposes in the lives of our children. This is what Rick wrote:

> In Colossians 4:2, the apostle Paul gives very good advice to you and me.... He explicitly tells us how long we should keep praying and what kind of expectation we must have when we pray. Then he tells us the kind of attitude we must maintain while waiting for the answer to

come. Paul writes, "*Continue* in prayer, and watch in the same with thanksgiving...."

...The word "continue" comes from the Greek word *proskartereo*, which is a compound of the words *pros* and *kartereo*. The word *pros* means *to* or *toward*, and the word *kartereo* comes from the word *karteros*, which is the Greek word meaning *to be strong; to be stout; to bear up; to have fortitude;* or *to be steadfast*. It gives the idea of something that is *strong, robust, tough, solid,* or *heavy-duty.*

But when *kartereo* is compounded with the word *pros* as in Colossians 4:2, the new word depicts *a strong, solid, never-give-up type of leaning toward an object*. It pictures someone who so fiercely wants something that he is leaning forward toward that object — *pressing toward it, devoted to the goal of obtaining it, and busily engaged in activities that will bring the object of his desire to him.*

This word *proskartereo* emphatically means that the apostle Paul is urging us:

❖ To stay forward-directed and focused in prayer.

❖ To keep pressing into the Spirit.

❖ To resolutely refuse to give up until we have obtained that for which we are praying.

I want to strongly encourage you as one parent to another: *Take these scriptural truths to heart, and then take your stand in intercession for your children and DON'T GIVE UP!* Press into the Spirit more than you ever have before as you proclaim to the enemy, "Devil, you take your filthy, stinking hands off my children in Jesus' name! God's Word says that the seed of the righteous shall be delivered [Proverbs 11:21]. These children are my seed, so *they are blessed and delivered!*"

You still have authority in your children's lives, even after they are grown, and it's up to you not to give up that place of authority with God. He is waiting for you to bring your children before His throne continually, holding fast to your faith as you contend for the purposes of God to be fulfilled in their lives.

Remember, the Father has a throne of *grace*, not a throne of *faith*:

> **For we have not an high priest which cannot be touched with the feeling of our infirmities; but was in all points tempted like as we are, yet without sin.**
> **Let us therefore come boldly unto the throne of grace, that we**

may obtain mercy, and find grace
to help in time of need.

Hebrews 4:15,16

So go boldly before that throne with
your children or grandchildren's names on
your lips, and thank Him for His grace and
mercy to help them in their time of need.
Take your intercessory role seriously, and set
aside the extra time you need to get in God's
Presence and fight for your children.

> **Set aside
> the extra
> time you
> need to get
> in God's
> Presence
> and fight
> for your
> children.**

You may lose some
sleep at times, but in the
long run you will have
gained more joy, strength,
and health as you see
your children and grand-
children serving and lov-
ing Jesus.

50

# Don't Waste Your Allotted Time

Take advantage of your season of intercession. I'm telling you, your season will come and it will go, so don't waste any more time!

## Time To Get in Shape!

Let's look at another example. Perhaps God is speaking to you about your weight, and you have been refusing to do anything about it. You may have been saying for three years, "I'm going to change my diet and start exercising," but you keep putting it off. Meanwhile, your risk for diabetes, hypoglycemia, and other diseases related to being overweight is growing stronger and stronger.

You may have been thinking, *Oh, well, I don't need to be in a hurry. My weight isn't a serious issue.* No, it *is* serious. If the Holy Spirit is telling you to lose weight, He is doing it for some very good reasons!

For instance, diabetes is becoming an epidemic in America because of poor diet. This fact hit home to me recently when I was talking to an American doctor, a blood specialist, who was visiting in Moscow. She told me that of all the babies born in America in 2004, one out of every four of them will have diabetes by the time they are teenagers!

Diabetes used to be just for old people. When you walked into rooms for kidney dialysis, you used to see only older people there. Now you'll see many children and teenagers too!

A few years ago, my aunt had to undergo kidney dialysis, and she was shocked to see how many young people were there for dialysis as well. Many were there because they had eaten too much junk food all their young lives, messing up their bodies until their kidneys couldn't function any longer.

# Don't Waste Your Allotted Time

So *pay attention* if God is speaking to you about your physical condition. If you know He's telling you to:

- ❖ eat less;

- ❖ maintain a more balanced and healthy diet;

- ❖ have more times of fasting and prayer;

- ❖ exercise more;

- ❖ or get serious about the health of your body —

*Then don't ignore the Holy Spirit!*

Don't say, "I'll do it tomorrow. I'll do it next week. I'll do it next month. I'll do it next year." The longer you put off your obedience in this area, the longer you sow seeds of bad

> **Pay attention if God is speaking to you about your physical condition.**

health and bad habits into your life. Soon a year will pass, then another and another. Before you know it, you'll be saying, "I want to get on the treadmill, but I can't do it anymore!"

We have to get honest with ourselves in this area. Too often we tell God that we want to give Him our lives — but then we won't even say *no* to that second helping when the Holy Spirit is convicting us! God wants to use us, but He wants to use us as *healthy* vessels to His glory. He also wants us to enjoy our lives to the fullest, but we can only do that if we live a life of obedience. Guilt is not pleasant, and disobedience always has consequences.

> **God wants to use us, but He wants to use us as healthy vessels to His glory.**
>
>

# Don't Waste Your Allotted Time

## Time To Honor Your Parents

Perhaps the Lord has been talking to you about the season of taking care of your parents in their later years. Sometimes this is a very difficult time, but it can also be a very blessed season of our lives.

You need to take heed to what God is telling you to do for your parents, for this is another precious opportunity that only comes once.

It's important that you do as much as possible for them when they need you in their older years. Look for ways to honor your parents for all they have done for you.

> **Take heed to what God is telling you to do for your parents, for this is another precious opportunity that only comes once.**

The Bible says in Deuteronomy 5:16 that your obedience to honor your father and mother results in the fulfillment of God's promise in your own life to honor you and give you a long and good life. When you unselfishly care for your parents when they are in need, you are sowing into your own future.

So keep calling your mother and father on the telephone just to chat and keep each other updated on your lives. Visit them as much as you can. Help provide for their needs. If Jesus tarries, one day *you* will be elderly, and you're going to want someone to visit and to be kind to you. You're going to want the telephone to ring. But if you never made your parents' phone ring, why do you think your children are going to call *you*?

Perhaps you have been holding offenses against your parents for many years. If so, it's time to extend mercy to them. Your

# Don't Waste Your Allotted Time

parents may have made a lot of mistakes in raising you, but they did the best they could at that time. And as you pour out love and mercy on them, you could be the instrument that helps mend their hearts. That would do a lot more good than just preaching to them. Let your parents see Jesus through your love and your forgiving heart toward them!

Make sure you don't miss your allotted time to obey God's commandment to honor your parents. As you lovingly serve them, God will fulfill His promise of good days and a long life to you!

Your life is precious, and what you do with it is your choice. God created you in His image. He's given you the power to do many great things and to affect many people for the good. But in order to fulfill what you were born to do on this earth, you have to understand not only God's will, but His *timing*.

*Do You Know What Time It Is?*

What season are you in right now? What assignment from Heaven have you been given to fulfill at this particular time?

As you seek to answer these questions, keep this all-important truth in mind: You have an allotted time for each season or assignment in your life, and only *you* can take advantage of that season by choosing to *act* on what God has asked you to do.

# 3

# Time
# To Show Love

Besides our relationship with God, nothing in life is more important than our relationships with other people. Yet so many times we allow the enemy to consume our minds with thoughts that steal our enjoyment of the people we love.

### Beware of 'Time-Stealers'

Let me give you a few examples of "time-stealer" thoughts as they pertain to our families:

- ❖ *If only my husband were like HER husband!*

- ❖ *If only my wife would do this, I'd be a happier man.*

- ❖ *Oh, my life is so terrible. I wish I had never gotten married!*

- ❖ *I wish our family were more like THEIR family.*

When you spend all your time thinking thoughts like these, you are wasting your time. You could be using that time instead to ask yourself questions that lead to actions that strengthen your relationships, such as:

- ❖ *Am I fully enjoying my husband [or my wife]?*

❖ *Am I taking the time to enjoy my children and to train them in God's Word?*

❖ *Am I pursuing peace in all my relationships to the best of my ability?*

❖ *Am I a blessing in the lives of the people I work with?*

❖ *Am I looking for ways to show those I love how much I appreciate them?*

The truth is, the most depressed people in the world are those who think about themselves all the time. They keep playing the same mental record over and over again, thinking about all the reasons their lives are not going the way they want them to go. The

> **The most depressed people in the world are those who think about themselves all the time.**

days, the months, the years pass by — and before they know it, the time allotted to these people to build strong relationships and serve others is gone. Instead of blessing the people God placed in their lives, they wasted all that time complaining and feeling sorry for themselves.

## Don't Withhold
## Your Words of Love

People go to funerals and say all kinds of nice things about the person who died. But did they say any of those good things to that person when he or she was still alive? All too often, the answer is no. People hold back their flowers and their words of love until their loved ones are six feet under the ground.

Our mouths should be filled with good things to say to each other. It's all too easy to think of what is wrong about someone else, but it's time that we stop taking the easy way of the flesh. We are wasting our time if we use it to complain and criticize. Those same moments could be used to tell others how much we appreciate them.

**Our mouths should be filled with good things to say to each other.**

Maybe your father never said he loved you. Perhaps neither of your parents spoke encouraging words to you. Regardless of your past, today there is a Lover living on the inside of you. That means you can determine, "I *will* use my mouth to encourage other people. I will speak good and kind words to others, even though good words were not spoken to me when I was young. I may not have been raised with good words, but I'm going to make a path for my children that leads to success through my words of love and encouragement and faith!"

You see, the potential we have for influencing others for good is *powerful*. But we have a choice: We can spend our time feeling sorry for ourselves. We can waste our time complaining or being offended. Or we can choose to make a way for others through words and actions that bless and edify those around us.

This is the key to making the most of our time and enjoying our lives to the fullest — giving our lives away in the pursuit of helping others. As Jesus said in Mark 8:35 (*NLT*), *"If you try to keep your life for yourself, you will lose it. But if you give up your life for my sake and for the sake of the Good News, you will find true life."*

## Stop Taking for Granted Those You Care About the Most

Too often we take our time for granted. We take our blessings for granted. We take our loved ones for granted. That's the way of the flesh — to take things for granted and to complain about what we don't have.

That day when I read the passage in Luke and the importance of *time* hit me so hard, I thought to myself, *I've got to go tell Rick I love him right now!* I wanted to tell my husband right then that I'm so thankful that we're sharing our lives together and that God has done so much through us as a team. I didn't want to wait till it was too late to tell Rick that he's the greatest man of God I know!

I'm not preaching doom and gloom in this book. I do believe we're supposed to live a long life and be strong until Jesus comes or until we've finished our course in this life. But we can't be foolish and just think we have all the time in the world that we want. One day the people we love are going to die, if Jesus doesn't come back first. Before that day, we have an allotted time to bless and encourage them with our words and actions, so we should be continually looking for ways to do that. For instance:

- ❖ Go to your spouse, "just because," and express your love for him or her.

- ❖ Do something special for your neighbors to bless them.

- ❖ Take the time to play with your children, giving them your undivided attention.

- ❖ Write a letter to a loved one who needs to hear from you, and let that person know how much you love and appreciate him or her.

- ❖ Make a phone call to someone you know who needs to hear words of encouragement.

I encourage you to take some time today to fill the ears of your spouse and your children with thanksgiving and praise for what they mean to you. Maybe they don't deserve a lot of praise at the moment, but that's all right. You're a mercy-giver! Those who give mercy receive mercy. So if you want to freely receive mercy in your life, you need to freely *give* mercy.

### Turn Past Mistakes Into Opportunities For Blessing

**Fill the ears of your spouse and your children with thanksgiving and praise for what they mean to you.**

Maybe you feel grieved because you didn't tell a deceased loved one how much you loved him or her before that person died. But you need to realize that your mistake is in the past. You can't do anything about yesterday, but you *can* do something today and tomorrow about the other people God has placed in your life!

Let me tell you about a Russian woman I know who illustrates this truth. Her name is Lydia, and she works with our women's ministry here in Moscow. Several years ago, Lydia had a husband and son whom she loved very much. But then her husband died of a heart attack, and Lydia turned to alcohol to drown out her pain.

Lydia gained newfound happiness when her son got saved and led her to the Lord. Then new tragedy struck when her son fell in with the wrong crowd of people, got back into drugs, and died of an overdose in the year 2000.

Suddenly Lydia found herself alone, a widow in her 40s with no children. She could have chosen to waste the rest of her life wallowing in bitterness and grief. But instead, she decided, *The devil took my son, but I'm going to do everything I can to keep him from taking anyone else!*

## Time To Show Love

Lydia determined to give her life away to as many broken-hearted, drug-addicted, alcoholic people that she had the ability to reach. She is the one who helped our women's ministry find a way to minister in the drug and alcohol rehabilitation hospital here in Moscow. I can't tell you how many hurt and broken women have seen their lives transformed because of the efforts of this one woman!

Now, consider what would have happened to these lost and hurting women if my friend Lydia had thought, *Woe is me! Poor me! I'm a widow, and my son died of an overdose. I'm just going to feel sorry for myself until it's time to go home to be with the Lord!*

Those women's lives may never have been touched by the love of Jesus Christ. They may have remained in spiritual darkness and bondage all their lives, never even knowing of God's love for them.

But instead, look at what Lydia has done through her obedience and her determination to use the rest of the time she has on this earth for good. She is affecting women for eternity!

So be wise about the opportunities that are given to you to leave behind the past and to serve others with the time you have left in this life. The day may come when you no longer have that opportunity. Some of those you love may not have the level of faith necessary to believe they're going to live long and strong on the earth. You just don't know how much time you will have to bless

> **Be wise about the opportunities that are given to you to leave behind the past and to serve others with the time you have left in this life.**

those who are closest to you. The clock is ticking, and you need to take advantage of every single minute you have been given to enjoy the people God has placed in your life.

## Steer Clear of Offense

It's possible that the very first thing you need to do in this area of relationships is to get things right with some of the people in your life. Don't let the enemy steal the relationships you treasure most through hurt or offense.

It's so important to keep your heart clear of offense, because it's impossible for God to do great things in your life when you have

> **Don't let the enemy steal the relationships you treasure most through hurt or offense.**

unforgiveness in your heart. Bitterness is an open door for the devil to come in and bring sickness and calamity into your life. Therefore, it's time to give up offense *today*, once and for all! You have time right now to forgive and to make the decision, "From this moment on, I am going to practice being the least offended and most forgiving person on the planet!"

We need to be that serious about our commitment to walk free from offense. After all, the Bible is certainly that serious about this issue. In fact, Jesus said that if we don't forgive others, our Heavenly Father isn't going to forgive us (Mark 11:25)! Any debt a human being could owe us is miniscule in

> **Don't let another day pass without getting all your relationships right.**
>
>

comparison to our huge debt of sin that was forgiven through Jesus' death on the Cross.

So don't let another day pass without getting all your relationships right. If you don't, the devil will just keep on eating up your time with thoughts of bitterness and unforgiveness. You can't fix those who offend or hurt you anyway. The only one you can change is *you*.

We must stop taking for granted our precious relationships, assuming that the people we love will always be there for us. It's our allotted time to forgive *quickly* and to make things right whenever there is a problem. And it's certainly the right time to show others how much we care!

# 4

# It's Time
# To Wake Up!

Jesus is going to return one day soon. He could even come *tonight*! The Bible says we're supposed to be continually watching for His second coming. We shouldn't listen to skeptics who say, "Oh, Jesus isn't coming anytime soon. It could be decades from now." After all, how can anyone know for sure when Jesus is coming back?

This is our time to prepare ourselves for the coming of the Lord by doing the things He tells us to do. The apostle Paul gives us a strong exhortation along this line in Romans 13:11,12:

> And that, knowing the time, that now IT IS HIGH TIME TO AWAKE OUT OF SLEEP: for now is our salvation nearer than when we believed.
> The night is far spent, the day is at hand: let us therefore cast off the works of darkness, and let us put on the armour of light.

These verses are still as true today as they were in Paul's time. Paul said that as Christians, we are supposed to "know the time."

But *do* we know the time today? Do we really know what time it is? Do we understand that it is *high time* to awake out of sleep and begin to pursue what God has called us to do with all our hearts?

Please understand — this isn't a message that is designed to bring condemnation. It's a message about taking seriously the time we have left on this earth. It's about waking up and making the firm decision to stop putting off the things we know we ought to do!

I guarantee you that the Holy Spirit is telling each one of us to do *something*. It's important that we obey Him and *not* say, "Oh, I have time to do that later." The clock is ticking. Time is not stopping. And God does give allotted times for the things He instructs us to do.

## Time Enough To *Obey*

As I was meditating on this message about time, an old song sung by the band *Chicago* in the '70s came to my mind. It's called "Does Anybody Really Know What Time It Is?"[1] The song talks about people who are always running everywhere, trying to beat the clock — yet they don't know the way they're supposed to go. They don't know where they are in life. They can't see past the next step or think past the last mile. The song concludes that we all have "time enough to cry."

As I thought about those lyrics, I realized that too many people in the Church fit the description of that song! These precious saints don't know or even care what time it is, and they just take it for granted that they have time enough to cry over the problems or obstacles they face in their life situations.

But we *don't* have time enough to cry. We only have time to put on the armor

---

[1]Robert Lamm, "Does Anybody Really Know What Time It Is?" from *Chicago Transit Authority* album, May 1969. http://www.chicagotheband.com/discography 01.htm

of God and walk before the Lord in the strength of His power!

That's the choice my Russian friend Lydia made. She decided that she didn't have time to cry about the tragedies in her life. So she stopped her crying and started sowing her life into other people.

I'm telling you, friend, it's time to take off the grave clothes that bind you and declare, "I'm *done* with self-pity and negative thinking! The Spirit of God is in me. Jesus shed His blood and went to hell for me for a reason — so I could do something great for God with my life! Nothing the devil has done or will ever do to me is bigger and mightier than the Spirit of God who lives inside me. From this moment on, I'm going to stop wasting time and start doing those things God has asked me to do!"

This is our time to call upon God and see Him move mightily through us to fulfill His purposes on this earth. It is high time for us to do what we know to do!

Friend, I'm just being honest with you here. In your future lies either a funeral or the Rapture. On that day when Jesus returns or when you take your last breath, that will be the end of your allotted time on this earth. You won't have any time left to say, "Just let me get my heart right first, Lord" or "Give me a minute to do that thing You told me to do ten years ago."

**It is high time for us to do what we know to do!**

Meanwhile, there is another inevitable fact you need to face. The older you get, the more your body will change and the more difficult it will be to maintain the high-energy pace necessary to fulfill your life assignment. That means that *now* is your time to pray. Now is your time to read the Bible. Now is your time to love people. Now is your time to obey God in *whatever* He asks you to do!

## Will He Find Faith?

In Luke 18:8, Jesus asked, *"…When the Son of man cometh, shall he find faith on the earth?"* Notice that Jesus didn't ask if He would find us doing religious activities. He asked if He would find *faith*.

One day Jesus *will* come back for us. But until then, He is watching us to see if we will take our time on this earth seriously and diligently pursue what He has called us to do, giving our lives in service to Him and to each other.

❖ If we bear fruit for the Kingdom of God;

❖ If we love Him with all our hearts and all our strength;

❖ If we give our lives to serve other people —

❖ Then we will not be ashamed when we stand in God's Presence one day, and we will gain rewards that will last forever.

That's why we have to change our attitude about time. Never should these words come out of our mouths: "Well, I have some time to kill."

> **Never should these words come out of our mouths: "Well, I have some time to kill."**
>
>

We have to wake up and begin to count our time as precious, for when the time is gone for us to minister to our loved ones, witness to our neighbors, or put the Word of God into our children, we won't be able to get that time back.

## Using Your Time Wisely

Jesus said, *"I must work the works of him that sent me, while it is day: the night cometh, when no man can work"* (John 9:4). Praise God, it isn't night yet! But what are we doing with the days we have left?

What value do you place on *your* time? Do you make good use of your allotment of time each day? If you find yourself in a situation where you are just waiting for someone to show up or waiting for something to happen, I want to encourage you to find a way to use that time wisely. Don't just sit there and let your mind wander aimlessly.

> **Do you make good use of your allotment of time each day?**
>
>

I have done that so many times. In Moscow, you can spend one and a half to two hours just traveling across the city to a meeting! This is a huge city with a population of 16 million, so in the course of traveling three to four miles, your eyes will probably scan 200 advertisements and 6,000 cars!

You can see how easy it is for my mind to be filled with all that I see around me and to wander in no particular direction as I spend those two hours riding in the car. But how wasteful it is on my part to throw away those two precious hours of my days doing nothing but mindless activity!

Recently the Holy Spirit has been convicting me about how I value and spend my precious time. He told me I needed to *make my time count* and instructed me not to waste a lot of time letting my mind wander. So now I keep a Christian book in my purse to read or I listen to a teaching tape while I'm traveling across the city. One day when I didn't have a book or a tape, I spent my time praying and cleaning out my purse during those two hours of driving.

We need to make the most of our time. Time holds priceless opportunities that we must learn to recognize and act on — opportunities to make something of ourselves or to serve someone else. There are just so many minutes in the day, so we need to take hold of them and keep them from just slipping between our fingers.

So make a quality decision to use your time wisely. Sometimes that will mean cleaning the kitchen, reading a book, calling a friend, praying and seeking God, reading your Bible, or memorizing a scripture verse. Other times it may mean exercising or just spending time meditating on all the blessings in your life. Whatever a given day holds for you, just make sure you do *something* in some way, large or small, that will bring more blessings and richness into your life or into the lives of others.

One day every one of us will stand before Jesus, and He will ask, "What did you do with the time I gave you? Did you use it to get to know Me better? Did you use it to help other people?" On that day, we won't have any excuses for wasting time. We won't be able to say to the Lord, "Oh, Lord, please forgive me. I just didn't have enough time to do those things!" And it also won't work to say, "Well, Lord, You just don't know how many problems I had with my family. You just don't know!"

>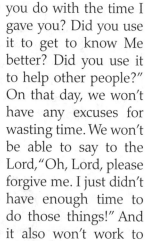
>
> **One day every one of us will stand before Jesus, and He will ask, "What did you do with the time I gave you?"**

# It's Time To Wake Up!

Jesus will just answer, "Yes, I do know. But what did *you* do with My blood and My Word? What did you do with the Spirit of God who dwelt within you? What did you do with the fruit of the spirit that I put inside you?"

When you look in Jesus' eyes on that day, do you want Him to ask you those questions? Wouldn't you much rather hear Him say, "Well done, thou good and faithful servant"?

What time is it for you, friend? Whatever season you are in, you can be sure that it will come and it will go. So make sure you're enjoying your season instead of wishing it away. Enjoy the people who are closest to you. Speak words of life to them. Tell them you're so thankful to God that they are in your life. Do the things God has asked you to do in the time He has given you, for surely He is going to come again.

You may say, "But it's so hard to live that way!" I understand why you might feel that way. After all, I'm just like you. I don't wake up with a smile on my face — I have to wake up and *tell* my face to smile!

When you open your eyes in the morning, realize that God has given you one more day. What are you going to do with that day? How are you going to start it? How will you fill the minutes and the hours? It's your choice. You are responsible for the choices you make in how you spend your time — not your spouse, not your children, and not your pastor.

> **You are responsible for the choices you make in how you spend your time.**
>
>

I urge you not to waste a minute taking your relationships or your time on this earth for granted. Every morning when you wake up, you should tell yourself: *This day has been given to me as a gift. So what kind of attitude will I carry through this day? What quality of work will I offer at my job? How many people will smile today because of me? How many people will be blessed by something I do or say?*

No one can decide the answers to these questions but *you* — and it will be the nature of your answers on a daily basis that will determine the quality of your life and of your time on this earth.

### 'Is There Fruit Yet?'

Jesus' parable of the fig tree in Luke 13:6-9 (*AMP*) gives us a clear picture of how God views a fruitless life born of endless procrastination.

> **And He told them this parable: A certain man had a fig tree, planted in his vineyard, and he**

came looking for fruit on it, but did not find [any].

So he said to the vinedresser, See here! For these three years I have come looking for fruit on this fig tree and I find none. Cut it down! Why should it continue also to use up the ground [to deplete the soil, intercept the sun, and take up room]?

But he replied to him, Leave it alone, sir, [just] this one more year, till I dig around it and put manure [on the soil].

Then perhaps it will bear fruit after this; but if not, you can cut it down and out.

One day as I was reading this passage, verse 7 struck my heart. The master said, "...*See here! For these three years I have come looking for fruit on this fig tree and I find none....*" Think about that! For three years, the master came every day to look for fruit on that fig tree without ever finding a thing!

Here comes the master. He asks the gardener, "Is there fruit on the fig tree?"

"No, Sir."

The next day, the master comes again. "Is there fruit yet?"

"No, Sir, not yet."

The next day, here comes the master again. "Surely there is fruit on the tree by now."

"No, Sir, there is no fruit."

A month passes — still there is no fruit. A year passes, and the master never misses a day to return to the fig tree and look for fruit, only to find nothing. He thinks, *Surely there will be fruit on this fig tree during this second year. I'll wait three months, and then I'll come back.*

Three months later, the master returns and says, "Oh, the branches on the tree are growing! Maybe there is some fruit on the branches!" But when he looks, he still can't see any fruit.

The sun keeps shining; the gardener keeps watering the tree. The master returns, thinking, *Maybe today will be the day.* But does he see any fruit? The answer is still no. Even though it's been two years now, the fig tree still yields no fruit.

The master leaves, thinking, *I'm doing everything I can for this fig tree. Surely there will be fruit during the third year.* By now, the master is wondering if the tree will *ever* bear any fruit the way it's supposed to!

Too often we're like that fig tree. The Holy Spirit deals with us in a barren area of our lives where no fruit for God's Kingdom has been produced. We say, "I'm going to deal with this someday. I'm really going to take care of what God is talking to me about."

Another day passes, and then another day. We say, "I'm still going to do that. I really am!"

A month passes; then another. Soon an entire year has gone by. We say, "This year I'm *really* going to take care of that. It's my New Year's resolution!"

But the truth is, if we have convinced ourselves that we'll eventually get around to obeying God tomorrow or next week, we're deceiving ourselves. We're just saying that to appease our conscience. If we were really honest with ourselves, we'd say, "The truth is, I don't *ever* intend to get around to doing that, even though I know

I'll bear the consequences of disobeying God in the end."

That's how honest we have to get with ourselves. We need to admit that we don't have any plans to do what we're supposed to do. Once we stop saying things we don't mean, God can begin to speak to our hearts and get to the root of the problem.

On the other hand, when we keep lying to ourselves over and over again, say-ing, "I'm going to do it. I'm really going to do it," time goes by and we don't change. We don't grow. The issues that held us back in our walk with God a year ago remain the same issues that are hindering us today.

That's why this message is so crucial for all of us. We have to adopt a different attitude about time if we're ever going to be all that God has created us to be!

# It's Time To Wake Up!

## 'Just Give Me One More Year'

Do you know what I've learned about people who continually say, "Just give me one more year to change"? They're not serious about changing. To alleviate their guilt, they deceive themselves into thinking:

- ❖ *I'll take care of that tomorrow.*
- ❖ *I'll go on a diet on Monday.*
- ❖ *I'll change my attitude next week.*
- ❖ *I'll get more disciplined next year.*

Yet these same people have no real plans to act on their words. So time passes, and they still say, "I'll do it tomorrow." Tomorrow comes, and they still don't do it. The next day comes, and their words are the same: "I'll do it tomorrow." The next month comes, and they say, "Oh, I'll do that next month." The next year comes; they say, "I'll do that next year." The next year goes by. The next ten years come and go. By that time, they're not even able to do what they said they would do ten years earlier. Their lives have changed; their responsibilities have changed. The time they had to do what they knew to do is gone. And all that time, they just kept making excuses and lying to themselves that one day, they were going to do it.

Let's not be like the fig tree in this parable — never bearing fruit but only depleting the soil, intercepting the rays of the sun, and taking up space. My prayer is that whatever God is asking us to do today, He won't be asking us to do the same thing three years from now. He won't be asking us in vain, "Where is the fruit on your tree?" What a tragedy that would be!

How do we avoid that tragedy? By realizing that there is a reason Jesus is telling us, *"Do it now."* He knows what is coming, and He wants us to take the time to be prepared for whatever is coming our way. That's why we need to pray along with the psalmist, "Lord, please teach us to number our days, that we might apply our hearts unto wisdom!" (Psalm 90:12).

> **There is a reason Jesus is telling us, *"Do it now."* He knows what is coming.**

# 5

# Choose the Best Thing

I have so much expectation about what God is going to do in the coming days! He is going to show Himself mighty to those who will seek Him. That is why it is more important now than ever before that we set aside time to seek God.

Anytime we direct our minds, our hearts, and our thoughts toward the love of God, we are doing the best thing we can do with our time. The seconds and minutes and hours we fill by lifting up our thoughts to Him always impart something back to us that can never be taken away.

To know God and to fellowship with Him is the greatest thing this life can offer. In John 17:3, Jesus said, *"And this is life eternal, that they might know thee the only true God, and Jesus Christ, whom thou hast sent."* No one can take away from you what you have experienced with God, for that experience was given to you by Him. It didn't come from the world. It came from Heaven, and Heaven will never take it away.

**To know God and to fellowship with Him is the greatest thing this life can offer.**

We can never spend too much time with God. We find this principle in Luke 10:38-42, which talks about the time when Mary and Martha invited Jesus over for dinner.

Now it came to pass, as they went, that he entered into a certain village: and a certain woman named Martha received him into her house.

And she had a sister called Mary, which also sat at Jesus' feet, and heard his word.

But Martha was cumbered about much serving, and came to him, and said, Lord, dost thou not care that my sister hath left me to serve alone? bid her therefore that she help me.

And Jesus answered and said unto her, Martha, Martha, thou art careful and troubled about many things:

But one thing is needful: and Mary hath chosen that good part,

which shall not be taken away
from her.

Luke 10:38-42

Martha was fixing dinner for Jesus,
and she got upset with Mary because her
sister was sitting at the feet of Jesus
instead of helping her.

So Martha came to Jesus and said,"Lord,
don't you see that Mary is not helping me?"

And Jesus answered,"Don't upset yourself, Martha. *Mary has chosen the best thing.*"

What was Jesus saying? *That we can
never spend too much time fellowshipping
with Him.*

### Take Time To Commune
### With the Lover of Your Soul

Now, I'm not talking about doing a lot
of activity for the Lord. Too often we scurry

around like Martha, saying, "I have to do this, and then I have to do that for the Lord!"

I'm talking about sitting at Jesus' feet with an open heart to worship Him and to receive whatever He has for you.

You don't even have to be in a "spiritual" place to sit at the feet of Jesus. You might be riding a bus or walking down the street when His Presence comes upon you. When that happens, even though you are in the midst of a crowd, at that moment you can have a meeting with God.

Sometimes God makes His Presence so real to me while I'm out in public, and I think to myself, *These people around me don't even know that I'm having such a great time right now. They don't know that the Creator of the world is talking to me!*

God is so simple. He's just looking for sons and daughters with whom He can have communion. He's looking for *you*. It doesn't matter what you've done or not done in the past. You just need to open your heart and say, "God, I believe You. I want more of You today than I had of You yesterday. I want to know You better today than I did yesterday." When you do that, He will be faithful to come and reveal Himself to you.

**You will *never* waste time by giving your time to God.**

You will *never* waste time by giving your time to God. So whenever His Presence comes upon you, stop whatever you're doing and say in your heart, *Lord, here I am. I'm listening. I want to receive from You.* As you yield to the Holy Spirit, He will begin performing miracles in your soul that no one else can see.

# Choose the Best Thing

The workings of God's Spirit in your heart are done in secret. As you enjoy times of private fellowship with Him, He changes you into another person — a joyful person, a free and whole person. It's that simple. All you have to do is open up your heart before Him anytime and anywhere, and He will be there.

Always remember this: *Jesus is in love with you. He is the Lover of your soul.* He loves you so much that it hurts Him when you don't spend time with Him. All He desires is that you open your heart to Him moment-by-moment and say, "Jesus, I just want to fellowship with You right now."

In Revelation 3:20, Jesus said, *"Behold, I stand at the door, and knock: if any man hear my voice, and open the door, I will come in to him, and will sup with him, and he with me."* This verse wasn't written to unbelievers; it was written to *the Church*. Jesus is continually seeking to fellowship with us through the Holy Spirit.

## Redeeming the Time

The Holy Spirit is with you right now, even as you read these words. He is moving in your heart. If you're worrying about a difficult situation in your life, He sees what you're going through. He understands. He knows your pain. Remember, Jesus bore that pain for you. He felt all that pain on the Cross and in hell so you could walk free of it. He doesn't want you to waste your time in anxiety and worry.

You may feel like you have failed. Maybe you've criticized and judged yourself for mistakes you made in the past. The Holy Spirit doesn't want you to do that. Jesus was judged; the guilt was laid on Him. He doesn't want you to carry that guilt. Your shoulders aren't made for that, but His *are*.

## Choose the Best Thing

If you have spent years carrying the burden of your past failures, Jesus has something to say to you.

> Come unto me, all ye that labour and are heavy laden, and I will give you rest.
> Take my yoke upon you, and learn of me; for I am meek and lowly in heart: and ye shall find rest unto your souls.
> For my yoke is easy, and my burden is light.
> Matthew 11:28-30

You may have wasted a lot of time in the past, beating yourself up over past failures. But Jesus doesn't want you to waste even one minute doing that. He desires to take that burden of guilt off your shoulders and to give you rest. He wants you to confess your sins to Him and then declare, "That's over. That's under the blood of Jesus! It isn't doing me any good. It's bringing my health down; it's wasting my precious time. I'm leaving behind the past, and I'm moving forward in God!"

That is the amazing thing about the mercy and the grace of God. Even when we have made mistakes that have wasted our precious time, He invites us to repent and start sowing great seeds for our future. *God gives us the power to redeem the time.*

**God gives us the power to redeem the time.**

My husband Rick once wrote something very profound along this line that I want to share with you. His words bring a note of great hope to this message about the importance of *time.*

This is what Rick wrote:

# Choose the Best Thing

Paul says in Colossians 4:5 that we must "walk in wisdom toward them that are without, *redeeming the time.*" I want to talk to you about that phrase "redeeming the time"— how it fits into the context of this verse and what it means to you and me.

The word "redeem" is from the Greek word *exagoridzo*, and it is the old Greek word used to depict *someone purchasing a slave out of the slave market*. It is a compound of the Greek words *ex* and *agoridzo*. The word *ex* is a preposition that means *out*. The word *agoridzo* is the Greek word for *the slave market* — a disgusting place where human beings were bought, sold, and traded like animals.

But when the words *ex* and *agoridzo* are compounded together, the new word pictures a *redeemer* who has gone to the slave market to

purchase a slave for the solitary purpose of bringing him out of that
place of slavery and restoring the
slave to the freedom he once knew.
Therefore, in this word "redeemed"
is the idea of *restoration* or *buying
back a slave from slavery*.

Now Paul uses this very word in
connection with "redeeming the
time." What does this mean? It
means that just as Jesus came into
Satan's slave market to do whatever
was necessary to break the domin-
ion of sin from our lives and
"redeem" us — buy us back and put
us on track with God's best plan for
our lives — now you and I must be
willing to do whatever is necessary
to "redeem the time" we have lost
along the way!

Yes, we can buy back time! Even
though it seems like an opportunity
has been lost, if we are willing to do

# Choose the Best Thing

whatever we must, we can often buy back lost time and make it right again!

The word "time" is the Greek word *kairos*, which would be better translated in this verse as the word "opportunity." So let me ask you:

- ❖ Have you ever lost any special opportunities along the way?

- ❖ Did you waste an open door God set before you?

- ❖ Did God try to increase your territory or influence, but you wasted your opportunity as a result of personal negligence or foolish mistakes?

- ❖ Did you squander an opportunity that God intended to be yours?

- ❖ Did you forfeit your testimony in front of unbelievers because of something unethical or unkind that you did in front of them?

❖ Did you lose opportunities to enjoy your children when they were younger because you didn't take advantage of the time you were given?

❖ Did you make wrong choices earlier in life, losing valuable time that could have been used to invest into relationships?

If your answer is *yes* to any of these questions, there is hope for you! Paul tells us that we can "redeem the time." Here is what that means for you and me.

Paul tells us that if we are willing to go the distance to do whatever is necessary to "redeem time" that has been lost along the way, we can buy back a lot of lost opportunities. However, just as Jesus lowered himself to the point of death to "redeem" us, we will have to lower ourselves to apologize to someone,

# Choose the Best Thing

to admit we were wrong, or perhaps even to make a serious correction to something we did in the past.

If you are willing to do what is right, you can *buy back* a lot of lost opportunities that you thought were permanently lost. Yes, it is a fact that you cannot turn the clock back. Time, once spent, is gone. But if you are willing to repent and to correct your mistakes, God has a special way of enabling you to *regain* a lot of time, opportunities, and territory that you previously thought were gone forever.

Isn't that wonderful to know? God is so merciful and gracious. He gives us room to repent and to start doing the right things with our time. And this we *must* do, knowing the time — that now it is *high time* to obey!

## Now Is the Time To *Prepare*

In these last days, we can know that God is speaking to many hearts. Of course He is — after all, that's the role and the ministry of the Holy Spirit! The Spirit of God is telling us to *prepare ourselves*. This is the season of preparation for the things that are going to take place on the earth.

I'm not trying to be dramatic, but the truth is, we don't know what is coming our way in the days ahead. Just consider the tsunami that engulfed the coastal regions of the Indian Ocean in December 2004. That disaster was totally devastating — a great tragedy for hundreds of thousands of people. However, the Bible says that these types of events are going to *increase*. The whole earth is groaning, waiting for the manifestation of the sons of men, crying out for us to come into our full maturity (Romans 8:19,22).

# Choose the Best Thing

So how much time do we have to waste by being offended or critical? How much time do we really have to complain, worry, or gossip?

In reality, we have no time for *any* of those time-wasters! Time is passing very quickly, and God is speaking to each one of us to do certain things. If we allow our minutes and hours and days to be consumed with any of these destructive pastimes, we may as well throw our time in a garbage bin!

I want you and me to be ready for God's plan as it unfolds in our lives. If Jesus comes in our lifetime, I want us to be able to say to Him, "I have done all I could do to fulfill Your will in my life." Therefore, *now* is our time to prepare for that day.

*So do you really know what time it is, friend?* Do you know that *now* is your time to do all you can for the Kingdom of God?

## *Do You Know What Time It Is?*

*Now* is your time to love God and people more and more every day.

*Now* is your time to get more serious about setting aside time to be alone with your Heavenly Father.

*Now* is your time to diligently:

- ❖ Correct your attitudes on a moment-by-moment basis.
- ❖ Forgive all who have offended you.
- ❖ Give away as much as you can.
- ❖ Live your life as unselfishly as possible.
- ❖ Lay your hands on people and pray for them whenever you have the opportunity to do so.

Now is the time to make the most of your hours, your minutes, and even your seconds, for the clock is ticking. One day you will stand before the Lord, and your time will be gone that was given to you to produce fruit on the earth.

So I urge you to *do what you know you're supposed to do.* Take this precious time to get ready for what is coming in the future.

Determine to become a ready minister of God, filled with His power and love. Use your time to the fullest! Certainly He is going to need you to speak life and truth and salvation to the hurting in the days ahead.

> **Take this precious time to get ready for what is coming in the future.**

Grab hold of every day as a precious gift, and learn to value even the breath that is in your lungs. The fact that you are still on this earth walking and breathing means that God wants to use you for His glory!

God has given Himself to us, and the third Person of the Godhead lives in us. Now it's up to *us* to take our place and live each day, each hour, and each moment to the fullest in Jesus' name!

# PRAYER OF SALVATION

If you have never given your life to the Lord Jesus Christ, please don't say, "I'll do that later." The Bible says that *now* is the day of salvation (2 Corinthians 6:2). You don't know what tomorrow will hold.

Just pray this prayer from your heart:

Dear Heavenly Father, I come to You in Jesus' name. Thank You for already providing me with my answer, for Your Son Jesus already paid the complete price for my sin on the Cross. Jesus, thank You so much for the terrible suffering You experienced for me.

Lord, I refuse to waste one more moment of my life in defeat and spiritual darkness. So right now, Jesus, I receive You as my Savior and my Lord. I humble myself before You to believe Your Word and to have faith that I can be set free through Your precious blood. Your sacrifice is enough for me, Jesus. You have set me free to hold my head high and become the person You have made me to be!

Thank You, Father, for forgiving me and for making me Your child. I love You, and I know You hear me. I pray this in the precious name of Jesus. *Amen*.

# PRAYER OF CONSECRATION

Jesus paved the way for you to be free to make right decisions. He paved the way for you to be obedient, because *He* was obedient.

So I encourage you to pray this prayer of consecration from the depths of your heart:

> Lord, You took the whole of my punishment and everything that represents death upon Yourself so I could be free to serve You. This is the day that I begin to make right decisions about what I do with my time. In Jesus' name, I come against evil spirits that have tried to steal my health, my call, my hope, and my very destiny in God! Father, give me a deeper understanding of who I am in Jesus. Give me a fresh revelation that I can do anything You ask me to do.

Don't let me make excuses, Father. Don't let me fool myself into believing that I don't have time to read my Bible or to pray while time continues to pass me by day after day. As the things of this world get darker and more difficult, I don't want to be unprepared for what lies ahead. So help me take a serious look at my life, Lord. Show me how to use this season to prepare myself so I'll be ready to minister to those who will be hurting and crying out for an answer.

Thank You, Holy Spirit, for Your power that resides within me. I purpose not to take Your Presence for granted any longer, but to fellowship with You as much as I can every day. By Your power and Your grace, I will start making the most of each day You give me, and I will do whatever You ask me to do! In the name of Jesus, I pray. *Amen.*

# ABOUT THE AUTHOR

 Denise Renner is an anointed minister, a mentor to women, an author, and a classically trained vocalist. She and her husband Rick reside in Moscow, where together they founded the Moscow Good News Church in 2000 and help lead the church today with their son and daughter-in-law, Paul and Polina Renner. Rick and Denise have proclaimed the Gospel throughout the vast region of the former USSR. Their ministry reaches a potential audience of millions in both hemispheres of the world via television, satellite, and the Internet.

# CONTACT RENNER MINISTRIES

For further information
about RENNER Ministries,
please contact the office nearest you,
or visit the ministry website at:
**www.renner.org**

### ALL USA
### CORRESPONDENCE:
RENNER Ministries
P. O. Box 702040
Tulsa, OK 74170-2040
(918) 496-3213
Or 1-800-RICK-593
Email: renner@renner.org
Website: www.renner.org

### MOSCOW OFFICE:
RENNER Ministries
P. O. Box 789
101000, Moscow, Russia
+7 (495) 727-1470
Email: blagayavestonline@ignc.org
Website: www.ignc.org

**RIGA OFFICE:**
RENNER Ministries
Unijas 99
Riga LV-1084, Latvia
+371 67802150
Email: info@goodnews.lv

**KIEV OFFICE:**
RENNER Ministries
P. O. Box 300
01001, Kiev, Ukraine
+38 (044) 451-8315
Email: blagayavestonline@ignc.org

**OXFORD OFFICE:**
RENNER Ministries
Box 7, 266 Banbury Road
Oxford OX2 7DL, England
+44 1865 521024
Email: europe@renner.org

# The Harrison House Vision

Proclaiming the truth and the power
of the Gospel of Jesus Christ with excellence.
Challenging Christians
to live victoriously,
grow spiritually,
know God intimately.

Connect with us on

 Facebook @ HarrisonHousePublishers

and  Instagram @ HarrisonHousePublishing

so you can stay up to date with news

about our books and our authors.

Visit us at **www.harrisonhouse.com**

for a complete product listing as well as

monthly specials for wholesale distribution.